Water for Everyone

Sarah Levete

www.heinemannlibrary.co.uk
Visit our website to find out more information about **Heinemann Library** books.

To order:
☎ Phone 44 (0) 1865 888066
▤ Send a fax to 44 (0) 1865 314091
▭ Visit the Heinemann Bookshop at www.heinemannlibrary.co.uk to browse our catalogue and order online.

Heinemann Library is an imprint of Capstone Global Library Limited, a company incorporated in England and Wales having its registered office at 7 Pilgrim Street, London, EC4V 6LB - Registered company number: 6695582

"Heinemann" is a registered trademark of Pearson Education Limited, under licence to Capstone Global Library Limited

Edited by Sarah Eason and Leon Gray
Designed by Calcium and Geoff Ward
Original illustrations © Capstone Global Library Limited 2009
Illustrated by Geoff Ward
Picture research by Maria Joannou
Originated by Heinemann Library
Printed and bound in China by CTPS

ISBN 978 0 431162 76 8 (hardback)
13 12 11 10 09
10 9 8 7 6 5 4 3 2 1

British Library Cataloguing in Publication Data
Levete, Sarah
  Water for everyone. - (Headline issues)
  1. Water-supply - Juvenile literature 2. Water resources development - Juvenile literature
  I. Title
  333.9'1
A full catalogue record for this book is available from the British Library.

Acknowledgements
We would like to thank the following for permission to reproduce photographs:
Alamy Images: Imagebroker 27l; Corbis: Alain Nogues/ Sygma 9t, Caroline Penn 11b, Smiley N. Pool/Dallas Morning News 16, Paul Souders 17t, Wendy Stone 27r, Peter Turnley 10, Larry Williams/Zefa 5t; Dreamstime: Bimuyu503 21c, Prasanta 7t, Istockphoto: Don Bayley 12, Bronwyn8 12–13, Esemelwe 23c, MvH 27, Nikada 3, Mikhail Olykaynen 16–17, David Parsons 18–19, Sean Randall 15, Fernando Soares 13c, Peeter Viisimaa 8–9, Sean Warren 29, Nathan Winter 32, Andrew Zarivnydam 21; Library of Congress: Arthur Rothstein 15t; NASA/ Goddard Space Flight Center 4; Photolibrary: Index Stock Imagery 18b, 20b, Oxford Scientific Films 22, Robert Harding Travel 19t; Shutterstock: 7, Mark Atkins 22–23, Bpatt81 6, Darrell Blake Courtney 11, Iain Frazer 20, Guillermo Garcia 25b, Ben Heys 7b, Robert Adrian Hillman 14, Tischenko Irina 5, Ed Isaacs 13, Muriel Lasure 1, 8, 9, Khoo Si Lin 26, Jim Lopes 18, Maugli 30–31, Vladimir Mucibabic 28, Nate A. 4–5, Oleg Z 22–23, Regien Paassen 24–25, Jeremy Richards 25, 25t, Ronfromyork 16–17, Vankina 10–11, Vuk Vukmirovic 28–29; Still Pictures: Hartmut Schwarzbach/Argus 15b.

Cover photograph reproduced with permission of Rex Features/Robert Harding/Duncan Maxwell.

Every effort has been made to contact copyright holders of material reproduced in this book. Any omissions will be rectified in subsequent printings if notice is given to the publishers.

Contents

Watery world 4

We cannot use most of the world's water 6

Getting water from the ground 8

Water can kill 10

Using water 12

No rain, no food 14

Climate chaos 16

Running dry 18

Dams store water; dams destroy life 20

Natural balances 22

Dirty water problem 24

Looking after precious water 26

Get involved! 28

Glossary 30

Find out more 31

Index 32

Some words are printed in bold, **like this**. You can find out what they mean by looking in the glossary on page 30.

Watery world

WATER IS VITAL for every living thing, from plants to people. In the developed world, most people take water for granted. All they have to do to get the water they need is turn on the tap.

However, many people in the developing world have to walk for miles to the nearest well to get the water they need. One in five people has no clean water at all. Drinking dirty water is one of the biggest causes of disease.

Where is the water?

Water comes in three different forms. Liquid water is the water you can drink. Liquid water also freezes into a solid called ice. It **evaporates** into an invisible gas called water **vapour**.

Never-ending cycle

Water is always moving from oceans to the skies and then back into the rivers and oceans. This never-ending cycle is called the water cycle.

About two-thirds of the Earth's surface is covered with water. This water is found in oceans, seas, rivers, and lakes.

Like any living creature, these elephants need to drink water to stay alive.

ON THE SPOT
Oxford

Oxford

A family is sitting at home in Oxford, Britain, eating a breakfast of cereal and apple juice. Without water, the family would not have any breakfast. Breakfast cereal is made from grain. Without water, the grain dies. Cows drink water so they can produce milk. Apples need water to grow.

After breakfast, the children brush their teeth and wash using water. They drink water at break time in school. After school, they go swimming in a pool full of water. In developed countries, people take water for granted. In other parts of the world, there is not even enough water to drink or wash.

We cannot use most of the world's water

ABOUT TWO-THIRDS of the Earth's surface is covered with water. However, all this water is not distributed evenly. Some places receive too much water, while others receive too little. The weather and the **landscape** determine how much water a place gets.

Salty water

People need freshwater to drink. However, 97 per cent of the world's water contains salt. It makes up the vast oceans that dominate the planet. Saltwater cannot be used for drinking or watering **crops**. Most of the freshwater in the world is locked away in **glaciers** and ice caps.

Groundwater

When it rains, some water soaks into layers of dirt, sand, and stone. The water collects in **aquifers**. People drill into the ground to get water from aquifers.

When the water in rain-soaked earth reaches the surface, springs or streams of water bubble up. This water in the ground is called **groundwater**. Rivers are formed from groundwater, falling rain, and the meltwater from snow-capped mountain peaks.

Expensive solution

Boiling seawater turns it into freshwater. The water **evaporates**, and the salt is left behind. When the **vapour** cools, it turns back into fresh liquid water. This process, called desalination, is costly. Many developing countries cannot afford desalination even though it would provide desperately needed water for their people.

✦ About 3 per cent of the world's water is freshwater. Nearly 70 per cent of this freshwater is frozen in glaciers and ice caps. The rest makes up lakes, rivers, swamps, and underground water.

BEHIND THE HEADLINES
Monsoon

Every year for several months, sweeping clouds bring heavy rainfall across parts of India. This massive rainfall is called a **monsoon**. For the rest of the year, India hardly receives any rain at all. Most of India's water supply comes from the monsoons. Farmers need the rains to feed their crops. If the monsoons do not bring enough rain, crops fail and the country does not have enough water.

A woman shelters from the heavy rains during the monsoon season in India.

About 0.3 per cent of all the freshwater in the world is found in rivers and lakes.

Getting water from the ground

MOST PEOPLE JUST turn on a tap to get all the freshwater they need. This water flows through networks of pipes and drains, from rivers, lakes, and **aquifers**.

Many people in developed countries take clean water for granted.

Cleaning up

Freshwater from rivers, lakes, and other sources needs to be cleaned before people can drink it. This gets rid of any germs or dirt in the water. In the developed world, water is cleaned in treatment plants. Chemicals are added to kill any germs in the water. The water is then safe to drink.

Collecting water

In the developing world, there is not enough money to build pipes and drains from rivers. Instead, people have to collect water from rivers and lakes, which they share with animals. The water from these places is usually very dirty.

Women and children have the job of collecting the water. They walk for miles in scorching heat to the nearest river or lake. They fill up buckets or **jerry cans** with the water they need, and then carry them all the way back home. A filled jerry can weighs 20 kilograms (44 pounds), so collecting water is a tough job.

✦ By 2025, the United Nations estimates that about two-thirds of the world's population will live in areas facing moderate to severe water shortages.

In developing countries such as Ethiopia, some children have to walk miles to fetch water from a well.

ON THE SPOT
Guatemala

In the Central American country of Guatemala, it is not very easy for many of the poorest people to get the freshwater they need. Water pipes and sewage systems were destroyed or damaged during a war that was waged in the country for many years.

During the rainy season, people collect rainwater from their roofs. When the rains stop, families have to walk for an hour or more to collect water from the nearest pond or river. Often the water is not clean, and it can cause serious disease, especially in children.

Water can kill

PEOPLE USE WATER to keep clean and wash away germs. After using the toilet, you flush it to wash away the waste into the sewers. Eventually, this waste water is cleaned. In some parts of the world, people do not have proper toilets. There is not enough water to flush away the waste. This means that disease spreads quickly.

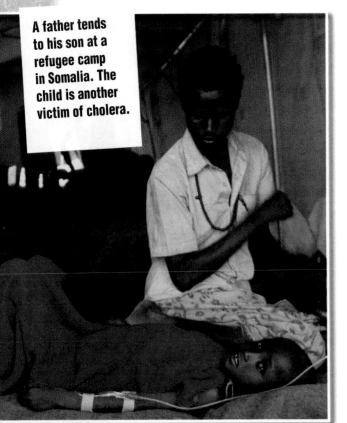

A father tends to his son at a refugee camp in Somalia. The child is another victim of cholera.

Wash your hands!

Washing hands gets rid of germs. The water flows down pipes where it is cleaned. Without clean water, germs stick around, and this makes people unwell.

Waterborne diseases

In the developing world, and especially in the countryside, the only available water is from rivers and lakes. This water is often dirty. Harmful germs cause diarrhoea and diseases such as cholera, dysentry, and typhoid.

Children and old people are especially at risk from diseases caused by drinking dirty water. Their bodies cannot fight off the harmful germs. Often there are no doctors nearby to help the children get well again. Even if a child recovers from illness, there is a strong chance they could fall ill again. They may be too ill to go to school, which can affect their future. Every year, two million children under the age of five die from the effects of diarrhoea.

FACT! ✦ People can live for weeks without food, but they can only survive for days without water.

BEHIND THE HEADLINES
Drinking water

More than half of the human body is made up of water. The body doesn't store water, so people need to drink about six to eight large glasses of water every day. Without enough water, the body does not work properly. This is called **dehydration**.

A woman from Uganda collects water from a dirty puddle. She runs the risk of catching many waterborne diseases.

Using water

WATER IS NOT just for drinking, washing, and cleaning! Water is used to make everything from the chair you are sitting on to the book you are reading.

Lots of water

Think about how many times you have used water today. Running a bath uses 7 to 12 litres (12.5 to 21.5 pints) of water a minute. Flushing a toilet uses up to 20 litres (36 pints) of water. A person living in a city in the United States uses about 600 litres (1,080 pints) of water every day. A person in sub-Saharan Africa uses up to 20 litres (36 pints) of water a day.

Farmers use water

Farmers use up to 70 per cent of the world's freshwater to water their **crops** and livestock. Without water, the crops would fail and animals would die, because they would have no food. Pipes drain water away from rivers and lakes to feed the crops. This is called **irrigation**. A farmer uses as much water as an average family uses in 10 months to produce one kilogram (2.2 pounds) of meat.

Farmers need water to irrigate their crops and grow enough food for everyone to eat.

Soft drinks factories are bad for local communities: Who is right and who is wrong?

FOR

Soft drinks factories divert water away from local communities. They use this water to make soft drinks, and local people are deprived of their water. They also release chemicals and waste that **pollute** the water that is available. Soft drinks are a treat. Water is a necessity.

Soft drinks taste good, but they often deplete water supplies in the places where they are made.

AGAINST

Water shortages are caused by lack of rain, not by the factories that make soft drinks. Factories provide work for the local community. They also help to build systems that increase the stores of freshwater.

No rain, no food

A HOT, DRY **climate** with little rain may lead to a **drought**. This means that there is not enough water to meet the basic needs of most people. In a drought, **crops** wither. Animals become weak. They cannot produce good quality milk or meat that farmers can sell.

Drought can quickly lead to poverty and hunger. Without enough water, some farm animals will die. Droughts usually occur in **tropical** climates, but sometimes they affect people living in milder climates.

On the move
When people cannot survive in drought-stricken areas, they often **migrate** to another area where there is more water. When people migrate, they settle on land that may not be suitable for farming. The soil may be weak and dry. Planting too many crops and letting cattle trample on this dry, dusty ground makes it even drier. This process is known as **desertification**.

Fights break out at wells
During a drought, people have to walk for days to find the water they need. People are tired, thirsty, and hungry, and tempers are short. Fights often break out as desperate people try to secure enough water for their thirsty families.

Dealing with drought
Drought cannot be prevented, but people have developed ways to survive and adapt to the hot, dry conditions. Small dams built across streams collect rainwater. The water behind the dam is known as a reservoir. It provides water for local communities when the rain does not fall.

Planting trees helps to store water underground, because the roots of the trees trap water in the soil. Fences made from rows of trees can help to prevent desertification. The roots hold the soil together and prevent it from turning into dust. Planting crops that need little water, such as cassava, helps to provide people with food during times of drought.

BEHIND THE HEADLINES
The Dust Bowl

A farmer and his sons run for cover during a dust storm at a farm in Oklahoma in the 1930s.

During the 1930s, the Central Plains of the United States suffered a severe drought. The farmers continued to grow crops. The soil became weak, dry, and dusty. The area was known as the Dust Bowl. Winds blew clouds of dust on everything. Improved methods of farming have prevented this type of disaster from happening again.

Modern-day refugees in Sudan walk for miles to collect the water they need.

Climate chaos

Human activities are affecting the world's **temperature** and climate. In turn, these are interfering with the water cycle.

Warmer Earth

The remains of plants and animals that lived millions of years ago make **fossil fuels**. When fossil fuels burn, they produce a gas called **carbon dioxide**.

Water floods homes in downtown New Orleans following the devastation of Hurricane Katrina in 2005.

Trees, plants, and the oceans soak up a lot of carbon dioxide. However, people are using too much **oil** and producing more carbon dioxide than the plants and oceans can absorb. This is causing **climate change** and **global warming**.

Extreme weather

Scientists think that climate change is partly responsible for the increase in **extreme weather events** such as **droughts** and floods. These weather events cause havoc and disaster around the world.

Crops wither and die when there is a drought. When **crops** fail, there is not enough food to feed livestock and people. Floods also destroy crops. Heavy rains damage pipes and drains. Sewage often flows freely in streets and into rivers.

Rising seas

The warm temperature is also melting **glaciers** and ice caps. Warmer water takes up more space so this makes the sea level rise. Some countries, such Bangladesh in Central Asia, lie near the sea level. They are at risk from sinking beneath the rising seas.

Global warming is melting ice in the polar regions, leading to a dramatic rise in the sea level.

ON THE SPOT
Malta

Malta

About 400,000 people live on the small island of Malta in the Mediterranean Sea. In the summer, tourists flock to Malta's sandy beaches. However, parts of Malta are in danger of being swallowed up by rising sea levels. The rise in sea levels is poisoning Malta's drinking water.

Salty seawater is seeping into the island's **groundwater** supplies. The government is rich enough to desalinate the water so people can drink it, but fossil fuels are burned in this process. This adds to the problem of global warming which will lead to further rises in sea levels.

Running dry

Filling up a swimming pool or paddling pool, watering flowers, and washing the car – all these activities use up a lot of water. When there is not enough water, many governments introduce water rationing. This means that people can only use a certain amount of water for certain activities. How do you think your life would be affected by water rationing?

Swimming pools

Winters with poor rainfall, and long, hot summers have led to serious water shortages in some countries. Stores of freshwater, called reservoirs, are drying up. From Spain to South Africa, major cities and busy holiday resorts are suffering from a lack of freshwater.

Barcelona in Spain is shipping in water from other countries to help provide enough water for local people and tourists during the hot, dry summer.

Wars over water

One of the sources of the snaking River Nile is in Ethiopia. However, much of the water from the river is diverted from its source and used to irrigate **crops** in Egypt. Ethiopia and Egypt both suffer from lack of rain. The precious water in the Nile is a source of tension between the two countries. Water is now so scarce in some parts of the world that people are starting wars to protect their supplies.

Swimming is great fun, but the pools use up a lot of water.

ON THE SPOT
Aral Sea

Rusting ships lie stranded where the Aral Sea once covered the land.

Ships once bobbed up and down on the waves of the Aral Sea. Fish once swam in its waters. Today, parts of the Aral Sea look more like a dry, dusty desert. Farmers in countries called Uzbekistan, Turkmenistan, and Kazakhstan took water from the rivers that fed the Aral Sea. They needed it for their cotton crops.

However, the effect was to drain the rivers and then the sea. Fortunately, the Aral Sea is slowly being regenerated. A dam on the Kazakhstan side has allowed the waters to replenish fish stocks. A new dam is being built on the Uzbekistan side. Work starts in 2009, and it will improve the situation even further.

Dams store water; dams destroy life

Dams are strong walls or barriers built across rivers. The dams stop water from flowing downstream. Instead, the water builds up in a reservoir behind the dam. It is used to irrigate **crops** or provide drinking water for people. Some dams are also built to generate electricity.

Power from water

The word *hydro* means "water". **Hydroelectric power** is the electricity generated by flowing water. This process does not create as much **carbon dioxide** as burning **fossil fuels** in a power station.

Dams destroy habitats

Large dams hold back the flow of swollen rivers. Building these massive structures has a serious effect upon local people and **ecosystems**. For example, there are hundreds of dams built across Snake River in the United States. The dams were built mainly for **irrigation**. However, many **species** of wild salmon along the river have died out.

Salmon **migrate**, which means they travel up and down the river. They spend up to five years in the ocean before swimming back to the rivers in which they were born to spawn, which means lay their eggs. When dams block their route, they are unable to complete the journey and they die before spawning.

Salmon may migrate thousands of miles to lay their eggs in the rivers in which they were born.

China was right to build the Three Gorges Dam: Who is right and who is wrong?

FOR

The Three Gorges Dam will produce electricity from water without adding to the problem of **global warming**. It provides the electricity needed by the growing Chinese population. The dam also prevents flooding downstream in the Yangtze River, saving the lives of millions of people.

The Three Gorges Dam will be the world's largest hydroelectric dam when it is completed in 2011.

AGAINST

Millions of people have had to leave their homes to make way for the dam. Around 13 cities, 140 towns, and 1,350 villages were flooded so the dam could be built. Damming prevents freshwater from reaching the sea. Fish **habitats** are ruined. Water seeps out of the sides of the dam and weakens surrounding hills. This causes **landslides**.

Natural balances

THE NATURAL FEATURES of a region help to regulate the flow of water within it. Today, human activities are interfering with the **landscape** and causing great damage to this natural balance.

Chopping down the mangrove forests

In some **tropical** parts of the world, such as South-east Asia, **mangrove** forests form a natural boundary between **rainforests** and the ocean. The trees have knotted, tangled roots, which are adapted to soak up the salty water. The roots also trap solid material such as sand.

The mangrove trees form a natural barrier, filtering the **sediment** from the river water before it reaches the sea. Sediment in the sea harms delicate **coral reefs**. However, 20 per cent of the world's mangrove trees have been chopped down for use as timber or to make way for land on which to build fish farms.

Building on flood plains

Flat areas of land that border rivers or seas are **flood plains**. These areas will flood if water levels rise. They act as sponges, storing and slowly releasing the flood water. Flood plains are home to a wide range of plants and animals. People are now building houses on the flood plains. This is risky because of the dangers of flooding. It is also likely to cause more flooding because the plains will not be able to soak up as much water.

Coral reefs are home to thousands of different plant and animal species.

It's not climate change, farmers are ruining the soil by overfarming: Who is right and who is wrong?

FOR

Many forests are being cut down to make way for farmland. Without tree roots to hold water in the soil, the soil becomes dry. When farmers also grow **crops** year after year, the quality of the soil becomes even poorer. Eventually it cannot support plant growth.

Vast areas of forest around the world are being cleared to make way for new farmland.

AGAINST

Overfarming and chopping down trees for farmland may harm the soil. However, burning **fossil fuels** is causing **global warming**, which is making the soil too dry. If we stopped burning so many fossil fuels, we could slow global warming. We should use less energy and burn fewer fossil fuels before blaming farmers. We need to grow food, but we do not need to burn so many fossil fuels.

Dirty water problem

FACTORIES AND SOME farmers use chemicals to help them produce goods and grow **crops**. Some of these chemicals flow back into rivers in the waste water from the factories or farms. In some parts of the world, the limited supplies of freshwater are full of chemicals. Drinking this water is very dangerous. Polluted water kills fish and other animals. One in six people depends on fish as their main source of protein. Many fish now contain dangerously high levels of chemicals.

Dirty water in the cities

More people in the developing world are leaving the countryside to live and find work in the city.

Thousands of people live beside the dirty waters of the Mekong River in My Tho in Vietnam.

They hope for well-paid jobs and clean water. However, there is not enough space for everyone to live in the city. Large communities of people build up on the outskirts. These are called shanty towns.

Too many people, not enough water

Water supplies do not meet the needs of everyone in the city. There are not enough pipes, drains, and treatment works to supply clean water. Waste water is not treated properly. It flows back into rivers and **pollutes** the freshwater supplies. As a result, drinking water is not clean. People do not have enough water to keep clean. Their health and wellbeing suffer.

Dead zone

Every spring, the rains wash chemicals from farms along the Mississippi River in the United States into the Gulf of Mexico. The chemicals are used by farmers to grow crops on the land. However, the chemicals encourage plants called **algae** to grow in the water. The algae use up all the oxygen in the water. Without oxygen, the animals that live in the water die. The sea becomes a "dead zone".

ON THE SPOT

River Ganges

The River Ganges in India is a holy river. Every year, Hindus come to the river to bathe in its holy waters. However, the river runs deep with raw sewage and poisonous chemicals. Many millions of litres of raw sewage flow into the river every day.

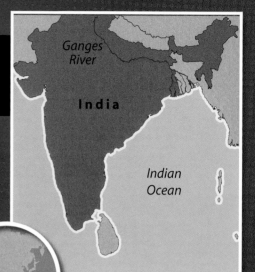

Ganges River

India

Indian Ocean

Crowds of Hindus bathe in the sacred River Ganges at Varanasi in India.

Looking after precious water

By THE YEAR 2050, there will be about nine billion people living on Earth. All of these people will need water. The amount of freshwater in the world will not increase, so we need to start managing how we use it now.

Losing water

Although water is in a continuous cycle, dripping taps and leaking pipes waste huge amounts of freshwater every day. Strict controls could prevent factories and farms from letting chemicals and other poisons leak into rivers. The controls will ensure that supplies of freshwater stay clean.

Catching drips

Rainwater harvesting is a way of catching rainwater and storing it for watering plants and cleaning.

In parts of Sri Lanka, people are suffering from severe water shortages. Purpose-built tanks collect rainwater. Instead of having to walk miles to collect water from a well, people collect water from the roofs of their houses. Women have more time for work. Children have more time for school.

Drip **irrigation** is a method of collecting water and applying it to the root of the plant, where it is needed. This stops the waste from other systems of irrigation.

Cloud-seeding

In a process called cloud-seeding, chemicals are sprayed into clouds to make rain. There is divided opinion about whether or not cloud-seeding is a good way of making water.

FACT!

♦ One drip of tap water per second wastes around 7,655 litres (13,800 pints) of water in a year – that's about 21 litres (38 pints) every day.

BEHIND THE HEADLINES

Plants don't need rain

Scientists are growing plants that can live in very harsh **climates**. They are mixing different types of plants that are adapted to different conditions. Some **crops** are designed to survive in very dry places with little water. Others are grown to survive heavy rains.

Creating plants like this is called **genetic modification (GM)**. Many people think that we do not know enough about GM crops and how they affect our health. Others argue that GM crops are vital to provide enough food for people where there is not enough water.

A girl fetches rainwater that has collected in a drum.

A farmer plants a seedling in the soil. He will use drip irrigation to water the plant and conserve water supplies.

Get involved!

What you do on one side of the world makes a big difference to whether poor people get enough water on the other side. Bottled water is supposed to be cleaner than tap water.

However, making plastic bottles uses up energy and adds to **global warming**. Making one 1 litre (1.8 pint) bottle of water produces 600 times more **carbon dioxide** than the same amount of tap water.

Bottled water is very popular in the developed world but making plastic bottles is adding to the problems of global warming.

✦ In the United States, 60 million plastic bottles are thrown away each day.

THINGS TO DO

- Leave a bucket outside one day. How much rainwater do you collect? Do you think you could manage with that amount of water in one day?

- Can you reduce the amount of water you use? Take a shower instead of a bath. Do not let the tap run when you brush your teeth. Ask your parents to put a brick in the cistern of a toilet. This will save 3 litres (5.4 pints) of water every time you flush the toilet.

- Be aware of how much energy you use. Using up electricity burns **fossil fuels** and adds to the problems of global warming. This affects the supplies of freshwater around the world. Instead of buying new things, try to reuse and recycle old ones.

- Design posters to put around your school that encourage everyone to save water.

Poorer countries cannot afford to build wells. Wealthy countries need to give more money to help give everyone access to freshwater.

- World Water Day is celebrated every year on 22 March. It aims to raise awareness of the issues around water for people and the planet. See if you can get involved.

- Encourage your school to find ways to save water.

Glossary

alga (more than one: **algae**) tiny plant-like organism that can make its own food

aquifer underground layer of earth and stone filled with water

carbon dioxide one of the gases in the air. Carbon dioxide traps the Sun's heat and leads to global warming.

climate weather that usually occurs in a place at different times of the year

climate change changes in the world's weather patterns caused by human activities such as burning fossil fuels

coral reef long ridges of coral made when coral polyps build their shells on the top of old shells

crop plant grown by farmers

dehydration lack of water

desertification process by which land turns into desert

drought long period without rain, when there is not enough water

ecosystem system of climate, plant, and animal life found in different parts of the world

evaporate dries up into the air

extreme weather event severe weather, such as a blizzard, hurricane, thunderstorm, or heavy rainstorm

flood plain flat areas of land beside rivers and seas that flood if the water level rises

fossil fuel fuel such as oil or gas that formed from the remains of plants and animals that lived millions of years ago

genetic modification (GM) adding useful features to a living thing, for example, drought-resistance to a plant

glacier area of thick ice high on a mountain or in the polar regions

global warming increase in the average temperature at Earth's surface

groundwater water under the ground

habitat place where animals and plants normally live in the wild

hydroelectric power electricity that is generated by the force of running water

irrigation taking water from rivers and lakes through pipes and drains

jerry can strong container used to hold fuel or water

landscape physical features of the land, such as rivers and mountains

landslide when part of a hillside breaks away and slides downhill

mangrove tree that grows in salty water along the edge of the coast

migrate to move from one place to another. Animals migrate to find food at certain times of the year.

monsoon season of heavy wind and rain

oil liquid that forms under the ground and is burned as a fuel

pollute make dirty

rainforest thick forest where it rains heavily almost every day

sediment bits of dirt and gravel

species particular kind of living thing

temperature how hot or cold something is

tropical from part of Earth near or on the Equator

vapour gas in the air

Find out more

Books

Save Water (Environment Action!), Kay Burnham (Crabtree Publishing Company, 2007)

Saving Water (Help the Environment), Charlotte Guillain (Heinemann Library, 2008)

Water in the News (Science News Flash), Yael Calhoun (Chelsea House Publications, 2007)

Water Pollution (Our Environment), Peggy J. Parks (KidHaven Press, 2007)

Water Pollution & Health (Health & the Environment), Cordelia Strange (AlphaHouse Publishing, 2008)

Water Supplies (Action for the Environment), Jude Welton (Franklin Watts, 2006)

Websites

The United States Geological Survey website includes lots of information about water and the environment. Go to:
http://ga.water.usgs.gov/edu/

Play games and take part in activities and competitions at this award-winning EcoKids website:
www.ecokids.ca

Find out about drinking water at the website of the United States Environmental Protection Agency. Go to:
www.epa.gov/safewater/kids

The Wild Over Water website has lots of interactive games and includes links and school pages. Go to:
www.wow4water.net

Index

aquifers 6, 8
Aral Sea 19

Bangladesh 16
Barcelona, Spain 18

carbon dioxide 16, 20, 23, 28
climate change 16, 23
cloud-seeding 26
coral reefs 22
crops 6, 7, 12, 14, 15, 16, 18, 19, 20, 23, 24, 27
   GM crops 27

dams 20–21
dehydration 11
desalination 6, 17
developed world 4, 5, 8, 28
developing world 4, 6, 8, 10, 24
disease 4, 9, 10, 11
drip irrigation 26, 27
drought 14–15, 16
Dust Bowl, USA 15

ecosystems 20
Egypt 18
electricity 20, 21, 29
Ethiopia 9, 18

flood plains 22
floods 16, 22
fossil fuels 16, 17, 20, 29

Ganges River, India 25
glaciers 6, 16
global warming 16, 17, 21, 23, 28, 29
groundwater 6, 17
Guatemala 9

Hurricane Katrina 16
hydroelectric power 20, 21

ice caps 6, 16
India 7

Malta 17
mangroves 22
Mekong River, Vietnam 25
Mississippi River, USA 24
monsoons 7

New Orleans, USA 16
Nile River 18

plastic bottles 28

rainforests 22
recycling 29
reservoirs 14, 18, 20
reusing 29

salmon 20
sea levels 16, 17
sewage 9, 10, 16, 25
shanty towns 24
Snake River, USA 20
soft drinks 13
Somalia 10
Sri Lanka 26
Sudan 15

Three Gorges Dam, China 21
treatment plants 8

Uganda 11
United Nations 8
United States 12, 15, 16, 20, 24, 28

water cycle 4, 16
water rationing 18
World Water Day 29

Yangtze River, China 21